Equatorial
& other poems

ALSO AVAILABLE IN THIS SERIES

Selected Poems

Adam / Adán
Square Horizon / Horizon carré
Equatorial & other poems / Ecuatorial y otros poemas
Arctic Poems / Poemas árticos
Painted Poems *
Paris, 1925 / Ordinary Autumn & All of a Sudden / Automne régulier & Tout à coup
Altazor *
Skyquake / Temblor de cielo
Citizen of Oblivion / El ciudadano del olvido
Seeing and feeling / Ver y palpar
Last Poems / Últimos poemas *
Uncollected Poems / Poemas inéditos *

El Cid / Mío Cid Campeador
Cagliostro
Three Huge Novels / Tres inmensas novelas
Papa, or The Diary of Alicia Mir / Papá, o el diario de Alicia Mir *
Satyr, or The Power of Words / Sátiro, o el poder de las palabras

Manifestos / Manifestes
Adverse Winds / Vientos contrarios

Volodia Teitelboim: *Vicente Huidobro — in perpetual motion / La Marcha infinita*
    (A Biography)

* *still unpublished when this volume was released*

Vicente Huidobro

Mirror of Water
Equatorial, Hallali
& Eiffel Tower

*El espejo de agua, Ecuatorial,
Hallali & Tour Eiffel*

Translated from Spanish & French by
Eliot Weinberger

Shearsman Books

Second, expanded edition published in the United Kingdom in 2024 by
Shearsman Books
P.O. Box 4239
Swindon
SN3 9FN

Shearsman Books Ltd Registered Office
30–31 St. James Place, Mangotsfield, Bristol BS16 9JB
(this address not for correspondence)

First edition issued by Shearsman Books in 2019.
This second edition adds further texts and contains a number of changes to the introduction and notes. The text of *Ecuatorial* in both languages has been re-set to accord with the 1918 first edition.

www.shearsman.com

ISBN 978-1-84861-819-0

Introduction and notes copyright © Shearsman Books, 2024.

Translations of *Mirror of Water*, *Equatorial* and *Hallali* copyright
© Eliot Weinberger, 2019. Translations of *Eiffel Tower* copyright
© Eliot Weinberger, 2014, 2019, 2024. All rights reserved.

Eiffel Tower first appeared in *The New York Review of Books* in 2014.

El espejo de agua was supposedly originally published in Buenos Aires, 1916, by Biblioteca Orión. It was issued in a new edition, privately printed, in Madrid in 1918. (See p.120 for further information on doubts concerning the veracity of the Buenos Aires edition.)

Ecuatorial was originally published in Madrid, in August 1918,
by Imprenta Juan Pueyo.

Hallali, poème de guerre was originally published in Madrid, 1918,
by Imprenta Jesús López.

Tour Eiffel was originally published in Madrid, 1918, by Imprenta Juan Pueyo.

The original texts of the poems here are mostly based on those printed in the author's *Obra poética*, ed. Cedomil Goic, Paris: ALLCA XX, 2003; the exceptions are *Ecuatorial* and *Tour Eiffel*, where preference has been given to the layouts employed in the first editions listed above.

CONTENTS

	Introduction	7
	EL ESPEJO DE AGUA / MIRROR OF WATER	
12	Arte poética / Ars Poetica	13
14	El espejo de agua / Mirror of Water	15
16	El hombre triste / The Sad Man	17
18	El hombre alegre / The Happy Man	19
20	Nocturno / Nocturne	21
22	Otoño / Autumn	23
24	Nocturno II / Nocturne II	25
26	Año nuevo / New Year	27
28	Alguien iba a nacer / Someone Was Going to Be Born	29
30	ECUATORIAL / EQUATORIAL	31
	HALLALI / HALLALI	
58	1914 / 1914	59
60	Les villes / The Cities	61
64	La tranchée / The Trench	65
66	Le cimetière des soldats / Soldiers' Cemetery	67
68	Le jour de la victoire / The Day of Victory	69
74	TOUR EIFFEL / EIFFEL TOWER	75
	APPENDIX: ALTERNATIVE VERSIONS	
86	Équatoriale / Equatorial	87
110	Tour Eiffel / Eiffel Tower	111
114	Torre Eiffel / Eiffel Tower	115
	Notes	120
	The Translator	123

Vicente Huidobro in 1917 and 1918

This volume is one of three Shearsman volumes devoted to Huidobro's publications in 1917 and 1918, all of which were originally published soon after his first arrival in Europe and his headlong charge into the avant-garde scene, both in Madrid and, more importantly, in Paris. The other two volumes each contain a single collection: *Horizon carré* (Square Horizon, written in French—although several poems in the first section are adaptations of poems from *El espejo de agua*) and *Poemas árticos* (Arctic Poems, written in Spanish).

This volume includes the remaining publications from that frenetic period and presents, at first glance, an odd mixture. Chronologically, we have *El espejo de agua*, written in 1914–16, allegedly first published in 1916, but, to all intents and purposes not distributed until 1918. I say "to all intents and purposes" because almost no-one seems to have seen the 1916 edition in Buenos Aires, which was then supposedly replicated in the first of two 1918 editions. The second 1918 print-run was a reset edition, and that is the one I tend to regard as the real first edition. *Espejo* is a transitional book, marking the end of the author's involvement with symbolism / *modernismo*—the end of that movement being definitively marked by the death in 1916 of its prime mover, Rubén Darío—and Huidobro's move towards the latest literary fashions in Europe, the latter undoubtedly one of his reasons for uprooting the family from Santiago and moving first to Madrid and then, at the end of 1917, to Paris. (The other reason, and almost certainly the prime initial impetus, was the public scandal arising from his affair with Teresa Wilms Montt in Buenos Aires in 1916.) Starting this book with the poem, 'Arte poética', Huidobro may be seen positioning himself for the post-Darío world.

Horizon carré, a large collection, follows and then come *Ecuatorial* (written in Spanish, although the author also made a French version, *Équatoriale*, which appears to be later, and is printed in the Appendix to this volume), *Poemas árticos*, *Hallali* and *Tour Eiffel*, the last two being composed in French. *Tour Eiffel* exists in two versions, one published as a chapbook on coloured paper, with artwork by Robert Delaunay, with another, earlier, version being a contribution to the magazine *Nord-Sud* (also in 1917); the poem exists too in a Spanish version, although this appears to be a translation by the Spanish poet, Rafael Cansinos Asséns.

These alternative versions are likewise printed in the Appendix to this edition.

After this torrent of publications, Huidobro slowed down, although he published a French-language selected poems, *Saisons choisies*, in Paris in 1921. The next two poetry collections after that were *Automne régulier* and *Tout à coup* in 1925, again in French, and significantly different in style, which were to remain the last collections until the astonishing explosion in 1931 represented by *Altazor* (supposedly begun in 1919, with the first magazine publications of parts of the poem occurring in 1925) and *Temblor de cielo* (written 1928). A further poetic silence followed, broken only by two volumes issued in Santiago in 1941, *Ver y palpar* (Seeing and Touching) and *El ciudadano del olvido* (Citizen of Oblivion).

Together with the experimental French poets, Huidobro was also quickly drawn into the group of expatriate Spanish artists—Picasso, Picabia and Juan Gris chief among them. Both Picasso and Gris drew portraits of Huidobro. The cultural ferment in Paris, the war notwithstanding, was something that Huidobro threw himself into. He would soak up the exhibitions, the music—he also got to know Diaghilev, the members of Les Six, and Edgard Varèse—the literary salons and café society. His work was marked by this forever, although he was to calm down in his artistic maturity after the great long works published in 1931. He was also to move into other spheres, leaving some of this poetic experimentation behind, writing novels and stage works, repeatedly founding magazines that quickly folded, while also finding time to join the political fray back in Santiago and, briefly, to run for President.

Like many intellectuals of his era he flirted with leftist politics, and joined the Communist Party—although he was to move away from it decisively in the 1940s. He agitated in Madrid in the late 1930s for the Republican government, against Franco's insurrectionist forces.

Huidobro's personal life also went through its ups and downs. During the early years in Paris he was accompanied by his wife, Manuela Portales—like Vicente, the scion of a Chilean upper-class family, as well as being a descendant of a renowned President—and their children, two born in Chile, and two in Europe. In 1928 he abandoned Manuela in favour of the barely-of-age Ximena Amunátegui, a relative by marriage, whom he whisked away from her boarding school in a dramatic escape to Argentina (with her connivance, it should be added, and the aid of a former family maid), whence the pair went to Paris. The couple had one child, Vicente's last. Vicente had fallen in love with Ximena in 1926, before her majority, and created a scandal by announcing his infatuation in a long poem that was published in the Santiago newspaper, *La Nación*. Their relationship lasted officially until 1945, when Ximena announced she was leaving; she then married a younger admirer, Godofredo Iommi (1917–2001)—an Argentine poet who had long been besotted with her. As the union with Huidobro had never been legalised, there was no impediment.

After a stint as a war reporter for Argentine and Uruguayan newspapers in 1944–45, during which he was twice wounded, Huidobro's final years were spent in Cartagena on the Chilean coast, with his third 'wife', Raquel Señoret, daughter of the late Chilean Ambassador to London and previously married to an English writer. He died in Cartagena on 2 January 1948, his end probably hastened by the effects of his war wounds.

Further Reading

Apart from the many Shearsman publications, these are worth consulting:

Vicente Huidobro, *Obra poética*, ed. Cedomil Goic (Paris: Eds. ALLCA XX, 2003.
Vicente Huidobro, *Poesía reunida*, ed. Vicente Undurraga (Santiago: Lumen, 2021)
Enrique Caracciolo Trejo, *La Poesía de Vicente Huidobro y la Vanguardia*. Madrid: Editorial Gredos, 1974.
René de Costa, *Vicente Huidobro: Careers of a Poet*. London: Oxford University Press, 1984.
René de Costa (ed.) *Poesía*. Triple Issue 30, 31 & 32 [a monograph dedicated to the work of Huidobro]. Madrid, 1989.
Volodia Teitelboim, *Huidobro, La marcha infinita*. Santiago: Ediciones BAT, 1993; 2nd edition, Santiago: LOM Ediciones, 2016. [Translated as *Vicente Huidobro — in perpetual motion* by Tony Frazer; Bristol: Shearsman Books, 2022.]

A single-volume edition of *El espejo de agua* and *Ecuatorial* was published in 2012 by Ocho Libros Editores, Santiago, in association with the Fundación Vicente Huidobro, albeit with no commentary.

A more exhaustive bibliography appears in the *Selected Poems*, also available in this series.

Tony Frazer

EL ESPEJO DE AGUA

A Fernán Félix de Amador, Poeta hermano

MIRROR OF WATER

For Fernán Félix de Amador, brother Poet

ARTE POÉTICA

Que el verso sea como una llave
Que abra mil puertas.
Una hoja cae; algo pasa volando;
Cuanto miren los ojos creado sea,
Y el alma del oyente quede temblando.

Inventa mundos nuevos y cuida tu palabra;
El adjetivo, cuando no da vida, mata.

Estamos en el ciclo de los nervios.
El músculo cuelga,
Como recuerdo, en los museos;
Mas no por eso tenemos menos fuerza:
El vigor verdadero
Reside en la cabeza.

Por qué cantáis la rosa, ¡oh Poetas!
Hacedla florecer en el poema;

Sólo para nosotros
Viven todas las cosas bajo el Sol.

El poeta es un pequeño Dios.

ARS POETICA

    Let poetry be like a key
That opens a thousand doors.
A leaf falls; something flies overhead;
Let what the eyes see be created,
And the soul of the listener tremble.

    Invent new worlds and watch your word;
The adjective, when it doesn't bring life, kills.

    We are in the age of nerves.
Muscles hang,
Like a relic, in museums,
But it doesn't make us weaker:
True strength
Is in the head.

    Why sing of the rose, oh Poets?
Make it bloom in the poem.

    For us alone
All things live under the Sun.

    The Poet is a little God.

EL ESPEJO DE AGUA

Mi espejo, corriente por las noches,
Se hace arroyo y se aleja de mi cuarto.

Mí espejo, más profundo que el orbe
Donde todos los cisnes se ahogaron.

Es un estanque verde en la muralla
Y en medio duerme tu desnudez anclada.

Sobre sus olas, bajo cielos sonámbulos,
Mis ensueños se alejan como barcos.

De pie en la popa siempre me veréis cantando.
Una rosa secreta se hincha en mi pecho
Y un ruiseñor ebrio aletea en mi dedo.

MIRROR OF WATER

My mirror, rushing through the nights,
Forms a stream running off from my room.

My mirror, deeper than the sphere
Where swans drown.

It's a green lake on the wall
Where your anchored naked body sleeps.

Over its waves, under sleepwalking skies,
My dreams send off like ships.

Standing at the stern, you'll see me singing.
A secret rose swells in my chest
And a drunken nightingale flaps on my finger.

EL HOMBRE TRISTE

      Lloran voces sobre mi corazón…
No más pensar en nada.
Despierta el recuerdo y el dolor,
Tened cuidado con las puertas mal cerradas.

Las cosas se fatigan.

    En la alcoba,
Detrás de la ventana donde el jardín se muere,
Las hojas lloran.

En la chimenea languidece el mundo.

Todo está obscuro,
Nada vive,
Tan sólo en el Ocaso
Brillan los ojos del gato.

Sobre la ruta se alejaba un hombre.

El horizonte habla.
Detrás todo agonizaba.
La madre que murió sin decir nada
Trabaja en mi garganta.

    Tu figura se ilumina al fuego
Y algo quiere salir.
      El chorro de agua en el jardín.

    Alguien tose en la otra pieza,
Una voz vieja.

        ¡Cuán lejos!

    Un poco de muerte
Tiembla en los rincones.

THE SAD MAN

    Voices weep over my heart…
Don't think of anything.
Awaken memories and pain.
Watch out for doors left ajar.

Things get tired.

    Outside the bedroom window,
Where the garden is dying,
The leaves weep.

The world languishes in the chimney.

Everything is dark,
Nothing lives,
At nightfall
Only the eyes of the cat shine.

A man has gone off on his way.

The horizon speaks.
Beyond it everything is fading.
The mother who died without saying a word,
Toils on in my throat.

    You are lit by the fire
And something wants to leave.
    The trickle of water in the garden.

    Someone coughs in the other room.
An ancient voice.

        How far away!

    A little bit of death
Trembles in the corner.

EL HOMBRE ALEGRE

No lloverá más,
Pero algunas lágrimas
Brillan aún en tus cabellos.

Un hombre salta en el sol.

Sus ojos llenos del polvo de todos los caminos

Y su canción no brota de sus labios.

El día se rompe contra los vidrios
Y las angustias se desvanecen.

El universo
Es más claro que mi espejo.

El vuelo de los pájaros y el gritar de los niños
Es del mismo color,
                    Verde.
    Sobre los árboles,

Más altos que el cielo,
Se oyen campanas al vuelo.

THE HAPPY MAN

    It's stopped raining,
But a few drops
Still shine in your hair.

A man skips in the sun.

His eyes full of the dust from all the roads.

And his song does not spring from his lips.

Day breaks against the windows
And troubles vanish.

The universe
Is clearer than my mirror.

The flight of birds and the shouts of children
Are the same color.
                        Green,
   On the trees.

Higher than the sky,
You can hear the bells flying.

NOCTURNO

　　　Las horas resbalan lentamente
Como las gotas de agua por un vidrio.

Silencio nocturno.

El miedo se esparce por el aire
Y el viento llora en el estanque.

　　　¡Oh!…

Es una hoja.

Se diría que es el fin de las cosas.

Todo el mundo duerme…
Un suspiro;
En la casa alguien ha muerto.

NOCTURNE

    The hours slowly trickle
Like drops of water down the window.

Nocturnal silence.

Fear scatters in the air.
And the wind weeps in the pond.

    Oh!…

It's a leaf.

It will be said that this is the end of things.

The whole world sleeps…
A sigh;
In the house someone has died.

OTOÑO

    Guardo en mis ojos
El calor de tus lágrimas…
Las últimas,
Ya no llorarás más.

    Por los caminos
Viene el otoño
Arrancando todas las hojas.

¡Oh qué cansancio!

Una lluvia de alas
Cubre la tierra.

AUTUMN

    In my eyes I hold
The heat of your tears…
The last ones.
You won't cry any more.

    Autumn comes
Along the roads
Ripping out the leaves.

What exhaustion!

A rain of wings
Covers the earth.

NOCTURNO II

    La pieza desierta;
Cerrada está la puerta;
Se siente irse la luz.

    Las sombras salen de debajo de los muebles,
Y allá lejos, los objetos perdidos
Se ríen.

La noche.

La alcoba se inunda.
Estoy perdido.
Un grito lleno de angustia;
Nadie ha respondido.

NOCTURNE II

    The empty room:
The closed door;
It feels like the light has gone.

    Shadows escape from under the furniture,
And there, far off, things that were lost
Laugh.

Night.

The bedroom is flooded.
I'm lost.
A cry of distress;
No one answers.

AÑO NUEVO

El sueño de Jacob se ha realizado;
Un ojo se abre frente al espejo
Y las gentes que bajan a la tela
Arrojaron su carne como un abrigo viejo.

La película mil novecientos dieciséis
Sale de una caja.

La guerra europea.

Llueve sobre los espectadores
Y hay un ruido de temblores.

Hace frío.

Detrás de la sala
Un viejo ha rodado al vacío.

NEW YEAR

      Jacob's dream has come true;
An eye opens in front of a mirror
And the people lowering the screen
Throw off their flesh like an old coat.

The movie 1916
Comes out of the box.

The European War.

Rain on the spectators
And a rumble of tremors.

It's cold.

At the back of the auditorium
An old man has wheeled into the void.

ALGUIEN IBA A NACER

      Algo roza los muros…
Un alma quiere nacer.

Ciega aún.

Alguien busca una puerta,
Mañana sus ojos mirarán.

Un ruido se ahoga en los tapices.

¿Todavía no encuentras?

Pues bien, vete,
No vengas.

En la vida
Sólo a veces hay un poco de sol.

Sin embargo vendrá,
Alguien la espera.

SOMEONE WAS GOING TO BE BORN

　　Something brushes against the walls…
A soul wants to be born.

Still blind.

Someone looks for a door,
Tomorrow his eyes will see.

A sound muffled in the upholstery.

You still can't find it?

So go then,
Don't come.

In life
Only sometimes is there a little sun.

Nevertheless it will come.
Someone is waiting.

ECUATORIAL

A Pablo Picasso

EQUATORIAL

for Pablo Picasso

Era el tiempo en que se abrieron mis párpados sin alas
Y empecé a cantar sobre las lejanías desatadas

Saliendo de sus nidos
                     Atruenan el aire las banderas

LOS HOMBRES
             ENTRE LA YERBA
                         BUSCABAN LAS FRONTERAS
Sobre el campo banal
               el mundo muere
De las cabezas prematuras
                   brotan las alas ardientes
Y en la trinchera ecuatorial
                 trizada a trechos

Bajo la sombra de aeroplanos vivos
Los soldados cantaban en las tardes duras

Las ciudades de Europa
               Se apagan una a una

Caminando al destierro
El último rey portaba al cuello
Una cadena de lámparas extintas

          Las estrellas
                 que caían
          Eran luciérnagas del musgo

Y los afiches ahorcados
               pendían a lo largo de los muros

It was the time when my eyelids opened still wingless
And I began to sing of far-off places unraveling

Leaving their nests
                       Flags stun the air

MEN
        LOOKED FOR THE BORDERLINES
                                            IN THE GRASS
The world dies
              on an ordinary field
Immature heads
                sprout flaming wings
Along the smashed stretches
                          of the equatorial trench

Under the shadows of the vivacious aeroplanes
Soldiers were singing in the hard afternoons

The cities of Europe
                Go out one by one

Walking into exile
The last king wore a chain
Of extinguished lanterns around his neck

                The stars
                      that fell
               Were glowworms of moss

And posters were hanged
                     along the walls

Una sombra rodó sobre la falda de los montes
Donde el viejo organista hace cantar las selvas

      El viento mece los horizontes
      Colgados de las jarcias y las velas

Sobre el arco-iris
          Un pájaro cantaba

    Abridme la montaña

Por todas partes en el suelo
He visto alas de golondrinas
Y el Cristo que alzó el vuelo
Dejó olvidada la corona de espinas

      Sentados sobre el paralelo
      Miremos nuestro tiempo

SIGLO ENCADENADO EN UN ÁNGULO DEL MUNDO

En los espejos corrientes
Pasan las barcas bajo los puentes
Y los ángeles-correo
        Reposan en el humo de los dreadnought

Entre la hierba
        silba la locomotora en celo
Que atravesó el invierno

Las dos cuerdas de su rastro
Tras ella quedan cantando
Como una guitarra indócil

Su ojo desnudo
        Cigarro del horizonte
                Danza entre los árboles

A shadow circled over the foothills
Where the ancient organist makes the forest sing

        Wind rocks horizons
        Lifted by rigging and sails

A bird sang
        Over the rainbow

    Open the mountain for me

I saw the wings of swallows
Scattered on the ground
And Christ took flight
And forgot to take his crown of thorns

        Sitting above the parallel line
        We look at our age

CENTURY CHAINED TO A CORNER OF THE WORLD

In the mirrors of the present
Boats go by under the bridges
And angel-postmen
        Rest in the smoke of the dreadnoughts

In the grass
        the locomotive that crossed the winter
Whistles in heat

The two strings of its track
Still singing
Like an untamed guitar

Its naked eye
        Cigar of the horizon
                Dances in the trees

Ella es el Diógenes con la pipa encendida
Buscando entre los meses y los días

Sobre el sendero equinoccial
Empecé a caminar

Cada estrella
            Es un obús que estalla

Las plumas de mi garganta
Se entibiaron al sol
            que perdió un ala

El divino aeroplano
Traía un ramo de olivo entre las manos

Sin embargo
            Los ocasos heridos se desangran
Y en el puerto los días que se alejan
Llevaban una cruz en el sitio del ancla

Cantando nos sentamos en las playas

Los más bravos capitanes	El capitán Cook
En un iceberg iban a los polos	Caza aurora boreales
Para dejar su pipa en labios	En el Polo Sur
Esquimales	

Otros clavan frescas lanzas en el Congo

El corazón del África soleado
Se abre como los higos picoteados

Y los negros
            de divina raza
esclavos en Europa
Limpiando de su rostro
            la nieve que los mancha

It's Diogenes with a lit pipe
Searching among the months and days

I began to walk
Along the equinoctial path

Every star
        A bursting shell

The feathers of my throat
Cooled by the sun
              that had lost a wing

The divine aeroplane
Brought an olive branch in its hands

And yet
        Wounded sunsets are still bleeding
And the days set off from the harbor
Carrying a cross instead of an anchor

We sit singing on the beaches

The most courageous captains	Captain Cook
Left on an iceberg to the poles	Hunts aurora borealises
To stick their pipes	At the South Pole
In Eskimo lips	

Others plant fresh lances in the Congo

The sunstruck heart of Africa
Opens like pecked figs

And Negroes
              of the divine race
slaves in Europe
Washed off the snow
              that stained their faces

Hombres de alas cortas
                  Han recorrido todo
Y un noble explorador de la Noruega
Como botín de guerra
Trajo a Europa
              entre raros animales
Y árboles exóticos
Los cuatro puntos cardinales

Yo he embarcado también
Dejando mi arrecife vine a veros

Las gaviotas volaban en torno a mi sombrero

Y heme aquí
          de pie
                  en otras bahías

Bajo el boscaje afónico
Pasan lentamente
                las ciudades cautivas
Cosidas una a una por hilos telefónicos

Y las palabras y los gestos
Vuelan en torno del telégrafo
Quemando las alas
              cual dioses inexpertos

Los aeroplanos fatigados
Iban a posarse sobre los para-rayos

Biplanos encinta
              pariendo al vuelo entre la niebla

Son los pájaros amados
Que en nuestras jaulas han cantado

Es el pájaro que duerme entre las ramas
Sin cubrir la cabeza bajo el ala

Men with clipped wings
                         Have overrun everything
And a noble explorer from Norway
Brought back to Europe
As the spoils of war
                     along with the rare animals
And exotic trees
The four cardinal points

And I too have embarked
Leaving my reef I came to see you

Seagulls flew around my hat

And here I am
             standing
                      in other bays

Under the voiceless trees
The captive cities
             slowly go by
Sewn to one another by telephone wires

And words and faces
Fly around the telegraph
Burning their wings
                   like inexperienced gods

Exhausted aeroplanes
Went off to rest on the lightning rods

Biplanes in labor
                give birth flying through the fog

They are the love birds
That sang in our cages

The bird that sleeps in the branches
Without tucking its head under its wing

En las noches
    los aviones volaban junto al faro
El faro que agoniza al fondo de los años

Alguien amargado
      Las pupilas vacías
Lanzando al mar sus tristes días
Toma el barco

Partir
    Y de allá lejos
Mirar las ventanas encendidas
Y las sombras que cruzan los espejos

Como una bandada
      de golondrinas jóvenes
Los emigrantes cantaban sobre las olas invertidas

MAR

MAR DE HUMAREDAS VERDES

Yo querría ese mar para mi sed de antaño

Lleno de flotantes cabelleras

Sobre esas olas fuéronse mis ansias verdaderas

Bajo las aguas gaseosas
      Un serafín náufrago
      Teje coronas de algas

La luna nueva
    con las jarcias rotas
Ancló en Marsella esta mañana

At night
> the planes flew by the lighthouse
The lighthouse dying at the end of the years

Someone embittered
> Empty eyes
Takes a boat
Casting his sad days into the sea

To leave
> And from there far-off
To see the lit windows
And the shadows that cross the mirrors

Like a flock
> of young swallows
Emigrants were singing on the inverted waves

SEA

SEA OF GREEN CLOUDS OF SMOKE

I wanted that sea for my old thirst

Full of floating strands of hair

On those waves they were my true desires

Under the gaseous water
> A shipwrecked seraphim
> Weaves crowns of seaweed

The new moon
> with its rigging broken
Anchored in Marseilles this morning

Y los más viejos marineros
En el fondo del humo de sus pipas
Habían encontrado perlas vivas

El capitán del submarino
Olvidó en el fondo su destino

Al volver a la tierra
                Vio que otro llevaba su estrella

Desterrados fiebrosos del planeta viejo
Muerto al alzar el vuelo
Por los cañones antiaéreos

Un emigrante ciego
                Traía cuatro leones amaestrados
Y otro llevaba al hospital del puerto
Un ruiseñor desafinado

Aquel piloto niño
                que olvidó su pipa humeante
Junto al volcán extinto
Encontró en la ciudad
                los hombres de rodillas
Y vio alumbrar las vírgenes encinta

Allá lejos
                Allá lejos

Vienen pensativos
                los buscadores de oro
Pasan cantando entre las hojas
Sobre sus hombros
Traen la California

And the most ancient sailors
Found living pearls
At the bottom of their pipe smoke

The submarine captain
In the depths forgot his mission

Returning to land
                      He saw that someone else was wearing his star

Feverish exiles from the old planet
That was killed on take-off
By anti-aircraft guns

A blind emigrant
                      Brought four trained lions
And another took a nightingale that was out of tune
To the harbor hospital

That boy pilot
                  who left his smoking pipe
Near the extinct volcano
Found men on their knees
                      in the city
And saw pregnant virgins giving birth

There far-off
                                There far-off

Pensive gold prospectors come
                        singing among the leaves
Carrying California
On their shoulders

Al fondo del crepúsculo
Venían los mendigos semimudos

Un rezador murmullo
                Inclinaba los árboles

        Sobre los mares
        Huyó el Estío

QUÉ DE COSAS HE VISTO

Entre la niebla vegetal y espesa
Los mendigos de las calles de Londres
Pegados como anuncios
Contra los fríos muros

Recuerdo bien
              Recuerdo

Aquella tarde en Primavera
Una muchacha enferma
Dejando sus dos alas a la puerta
Entraba al sanatorio

Aquella misma noche
                bajo el cielo oblongo
Diez Zeppelines vinieron a París
Y un cazador de jabalís
Dejó sangrando siete
Sobre el alba agreste

Entre la nube que rozaba el techo

Un reloj verde

              Anuncia el año

1917

Half-mute beggars came
Through the depths of twilight

The murmur of someone praying
                            Bowed the trees over

            Summertime fled
            Over the seas

WHAT THINGS I'VE SEEN

In the thick and vegetal fog
Beggars on the streets of London
Stuck like posters
Against the frigid walls

I remember it well
                      I remember

That afternoon in Spring
A girl who was ill
Left her two wings at the door
And went into the sanatorium

That same night
                under the oblong sky
Ten Zeppelins arrived in Paris
And a hunter of wild boars
Left seven bleeding
In the country dawn

In the cloud that brushes the roof

A green clock

                      Announces the year

1917

LLUEVE

                                    Bajo el agua
                                    Enterraban los muertos
             Alguien que lloraba
             Hacía caer las hojas

Signos hay en el cielo
Dice el astrólogo barbudo
                            Una manzana y una estrella
                            Picotean los búhos

Marte
            pasa a través de
                          Sagitario

SALE LA LUNA

                              Un astro maltratado
                              Se desliza

Astrólogos de mitras puntiagudas
De sus barbas caían copos de ceniza

Y heme aquí
                    Entre las selvas afinadas
Más sabiamente que las viejas arpas

En la casa
          que cuelga del vacío
Cansados de buscar
                    los Reyes Magos se han dormido

Los ascensores descansan en cuclillas

Y en todas las alcobas
Cada vez que da la hora

IT'S RAINING

                                        They buried the dead
                                        Underwater
                 Someone weeping
                 Made the leaves fall

There are signs in the sky
Says the bearded astrologer
                          Owls are pecking
                          An apple and a star

Mars
        passes through
                Sagittarius

THE MOON COMES OUT

                            A mistreated star
                            Slips away

Flakes of ashes fell from the beards
Of astrologers in pointy miters

And here I am
                In forests
More expertly tuned than old harps

In the house
            that hangs in the void
Tired of searching
                the Three Kings have gone to sleep

Elevators squatting doze

And in every bedroom
When it strikes the hour

Salía del reloj un paje serio
Como a decir
           El coche aguarda
                        mi señora

Junto a la puerta viva
El negro esclavo
           abre la boca prestamente
Para el amo pianista
Que hace cantar sus dientes

Esta tarde yo he visto
Los últimos afiches fonográficos
Era una confusión de gritos
Y cantos tan diversos
Como en los puertos extranjeros

Los hombres de mañana
Vendrán a descifrar los jeroglíficos
Que dejamos ahora
Escritos al revés
Entre los hierros de la Torre Eiffel

Llegamos al final de la refriega
Mi reloj perdió todas sus horas

Yo te recorro lentamente
Siglo cortado en dos
                Y con un puente
Sobre un río sangriento
Camino de Occidente

Una tarde
        al fondo de la vida
Pasaba un horizonte de camellos
En sus espaldas mudas
Entre dos pirámides huesudas
Los hombres del Egipto
Lloran como los nuevos cocodrilos

A reliable bellhop comes out of the clock
As if to say
        The car is waiting
                      Madam

Next to the open door
The negro slave
            quickly opens his mouth
For the master pianist
Who can make his teeth sing

This afternoon I've seen
The latest phonographic notices
A riot of screams
And songs as sundry
As those in foreign ports

The men of tomorrow
Will decipher the hieroglyphs
We've left
Written backwards
On the girders of the Eiffel Tower

We've reached the end of the skirmish
My watch lost its time

I travel slowly through you
Century cut in half
            And on a bridge
Over a bloody river
I walk from the West

One afternoon
           deep in life
A horizon of camels passed by
On their mute backs
Between two bony pyramids
The men of Egypt
Weep like newborn crocodiles

Y los santos en tren
                buscando otras regiones
Bajaban y subían en todas las estaciones

Mi alma hermana de los trenes

        Un tren puede rezarse como un rosario
        La cruz humeante perfumaba los llanos

Henos aquí viajando entre los santos

El tren es un trozo de la ciudad que se aleja

El anunciador de estaciones
Ha gritado
                Primavera
                Al lado izquierdo
                      30 minutos

Pasa el tren lleno de flores y de frutos

El Niágara ha mojado mis cabellos
Y una neblina nace en torno de ellos

Los ríos
      Todos los ríos de las nacientes cabelleras
Los ríos mal trenzados
Que los ardientes veranos han besado

Un paquebot perdido costeaba
Las islas de oro de la Vía Láctea

La cordillera Andina
                Veloz como un convoy
Atraviesa la América Latina.

El Amor
                El Amor

On the train the saints
                        looking for other territories
Get on and off at every station

My sister soul of the trains

          A train can pray to itself like a rosary
          The smoking cross that perfumed the plains

Here we are traveling with saints

A train is a piece of the city that pushes off

The conductor
Shouted
                        Spring
                        Exit on the left
                            30 minutes

The train goes by full of flowers and fruit

Niagara Falls has drenched my hair
And a mist rises around it

The rivers
        All the rivers of rising hair
The badly braided rivers
That burning summers have kissed

A lost steamer was coasting along
The golden islands of the Milky Way

The Andes mountains
                    Swift as a convoy
Crosses Latin America

Love
                        Love

En pocos sitios lo he encontrado
Y todos los ríos no explorados
Bajo mis brazos han pasado

Una mañana
                Pastores alpinistas
Tocaban el violín sobre la Suiza

Y en la estrella vecina
Aquel que no tenía manos
Con las alas tocaba el piano
Siglo embarcado en aeroplanos ebrios

A DONDE IRÁS

Caminando al destierro
El último rey portaba al cuello
Una cadena de Lámparas extintas

Y ayer vi muerta entre las rosas
La amatista de Roma

ALFA
                              OMEGA

                DILUVIO
                                        ARCO IRIS

Cuántas veces la vida habrá recomendado

Quién dirá todo lo que en un astro ha pasado

                Sigamos nuestra marcha
                Llevando la cabeza madura entre las manos

In few places I've found it
All the unexplored rivers
Have passed beneath my hands

One morning
                Mountaineer shepherds
Played the violin over Switzerland

And on the star next door
The one who had no hands
Played the piano with his wings
Century embarked on drunken aeroplanes

WHERE ARE YOU GOING

Walking into exile
The last king wore a chain of extinguished lanterns
Around his neck

And yesterday I saw the amethyst of Rome
Dead among the roses

ALPHA
                                    OMEGA

                FLOOD
                                            RAINBOW

How many times will life have to begin again

Who will tell everything that has happened on a star

                We continue our march
                Carrying the ripened head in our hands

EL RUISEÑOR MECÁNICO HA CANTADO

Aquella multitud de manos ásperas
Lleva coronas funerarias
Hacia los campos de batalla

    Alguien pasó perdido en su cigarro

QUIÉN ES

Una mano cortada
Dejó sobre los mármoles
La línea Ecuatorial recién brotada

Siglo
        Sumérgete en el sol
Cuando en la tarde
        Aterrice en un campo de aviación

Hacía el solo aeroplano
Que cantará un día en el azul
Se alzará de los altos
Una bandada de manos

CRUZ DEL SUR

SUPREMO SIGNO   AVIÓN DE CRISTO

El niño sonrosado de las alas desnudas
Vendrá con el clarín entre dedos
El clarín aún fresco que anuncia
El Fin del Universo

THE MECHANICAL NIGHTINGALE HAS SUNG

That throng of rough hands
Carrying funeral wreaths
To the battlefields

    Someone went by lost in his cigar

WHO IS IT

A severed hand
Left the new equatorial line
On the marble

Century
    Sink into the sun
When in the evening
    It lands at the airfield

A flock of hands
Will rise from the years
Toward the one aeroplane
That will sing someday in the blue

THE SOUTHERN CROSS

THE SUPREME SIGN   THE CHRIST AIRLINER

The rosy child with bare wings
Will come with his bugle in his hands
The brand-new bugle that heralds
The End of the Universe

HALLALI

poème de guerre

A mon ami Marius André

HALLALI

a poem of the war

For my friend Marius André

1914

Nuages sur le jet d'eau d'été
      La nuit
            Toutes les tours de l'Europe se parlaient en secret

Tout d'un coup un œil s'ouvre
La corne de la lune crie

Hallali
                                      Hallali
Les tours sont des clairons pendus

AOÛT 1914
            C'est la vendange des frontières

Derrière l'horizon il se passe quelque chose
            Au gibet de l'Aurore toutes les villes sont pendues
              Les villes qui fument comme des pipes

Hallali
                                      Hallali
Et ce n'est pas une chanson
                Les hommes s'en vont

1914

Clouds over the fountain of summer
    Night
            All the towers of Europe trading secrets

Suddenly an eye opens
The horn of the moon blasts

Hallali
            Hallali
The towers are bugles swinging

AUGUST 1914
            A vintage year for frontiers

Something's happening beyond the horizon
        All the cities swinging from the gallows of dawn
           The cities smoking like pipes

Hallali
            Hallali
And it's not a song
            The men go off

LES VILLES

Dans les villes
On parle
           On parle
Mais on ne dit rien

La terre nue roule encore
Et même les pierres crient

Soldats vêtus de nuages bleues
                                Le ciel vieilli entre les mains
                                Et la chanson dans la tranchée

Les trains s'en vont sur des cordes parallèles
                                On pleure dans toutes les gares

Le premier tué a été un poète
On a vu un oiseau s'échapper de sa blessure

L'aéroplane blanc de neige
Gronde parmi les colombes du soir

Un jour
        il s'était égaré dans la fumée des cigares

    Nuées des usines   Nuées du ciel

                C'est un trompe-l'œil

THE CITIES

In the cities
They talk
                They talk
And don't say a thing

The bare earth still turns
And even the rocks cry

Soldiers dressed in blue clouds
                              The sky grows old between their hands
                              And the song in the trenches

The trains go off on their parallel ropes

                              There's weeping at every station

The first to be killed was a poet
A bird was seen flying from his wound

An aeroplane white as snow
Roars through the evening doves

One day
              it was got lost in the smoke of cigars

      The haze of the factories   The haze of the sky

                      It's a trompe-l'œil

Les blessures des aviateurs saignent dans toutes les étoiles

Un cri d'angoisse
S'est noyé dans les brouillards
Et un enfant à genoux
      Lève les mains

   TOUTES LES MÈRES DU MONDE PLEURENT

The wounds of aviators bleed over the stars

A cry of pain
Drowns in the mist
And a child on his knees
                Lifts his hands

      ALL THE MOTHERS OF THE WORLD WEEP

LA TRANCHÉE

Sur le canon
Un rossignol chantait

                  J'ai perdu mon violon
La tranchée
Fait le tour de la Terre
           Quel froid
                      Tous les pères habillés en soldats

On siffle derrière sa propre vie

CRAONNE
                VERDUN
                                ALSACE

                C'est une belle cible la lune

L'ombre d'un soldat
Etait tombée dans un trou

      On voit par terre sanglant
      L'aviateur qui se cogna la tête contre une étoile éteinte

Et mieux qu'un chien
Le canon surveille
               Quelques fois
               Il aboie
                        LA LUNE

Toutes les étoiles sont des trous d'obus

THE TRENCH

On the cannon
A nightingale sang

                I've lost my violin
The trench
Goes around the world
                It's so cold
                            Every father dressed like a soldier

Whistling for his life

CRAONNE
                      VERDUN
                                    ALSACE

                    What a lovely target is the moon

The shadow of a soldier
Fallen into a pit

      Seen on the bloody ground
      An aviator who smashed his head on a burnt-out star

Better than a dog
The cannon keeps watch
                Sometimes
                Howling
                            THE MOON

Every star a shell hole

LE CIMETIÈRE DES SOLDATS

L'ombre qui tombe des arbres
S'est mouillée dans l'eau

        On ne voit pas le vent

                Mais la forêt métallique
                Chante comme un orgue

La voilà
      La France d'hier sous l'herbe
      Plus belle qu'une femme nue

La terre encore tiède
Garde les derniers secrets

        Où sont toutes les mains coupées

Une cloche sonne
Derrière les nuages

                Tournée vers l'océan filial
                Elle appelait quelqu'un

SILENCE
                      SILENCE

SOLDIERS' CEMETERY

The shadow that falls from the trees
Is drenched in the water

        The wind can't be seen

                But the forest of metal
                Sings like an organ

There it is
        The France of yesterday under grass
        More beautiful than a naked woman

The earth still warm
Guards its last secrets

        Where the severed hands all are

A clock strikes
Behind the clouds

                Facing the filial ocean
                It calls out to someone

SILENCE
                              SILENCE

LE JOUR DE LA VICTOIRE

Un jour la Paix viendra
                                        Torche au fond du siècle
Alors les soldats   les yeux pleins de pluie
Regagneront Paris

      UN OISEAU CHANTERA SUR L'ARC DE TRIOMPHE

Et le retour
Éclairera toutes les fenêtres

Avions
                            Soldats
                                                        Canons

Même les aveugles
Sortiront aux balcons

Et leurs fleurs tomberont aussi sur les têtes des soldats

Le cortège viendra des siècles plus lointains
La foule dansera dans les yeux des chevaux

            Un cri s'élève comme une étincelle
            Et les chapeaux monteront dans l'air
            Mieux que les houles dans les jets d'eaux

Avions
                            Soldats
                                                        Canons

THE DAY OF VICTORY

One day Peace will come
                                  Torchlight in the depths of the century
And the soldiers   eyes full of rain
Will go back to Paris

      A BIRD WILL SING ON THE ARC DE TRIOMPHE

And homecoming
Will light the windows

Planes
                      Soldiers
                                          Cannons

Even the blind
Will come out on the balconies

And their flowers too will fall on the heads of soldiers

The cortège will come from distant ages
The crowds will dance in the horses' eyes

        A shout will go up like a flash of light
        And hats will shoot into the air
        Like the balls at the tip of a fountain

Planes
                      Soldiers
                                          Cannons

LES AÉROPLANES   LES AÉROPLANES

Ne fermeront pas leurs ailes tout ce matin

LES AÉROPLANES   LES AÉROPLANES

De quel cimetière de héros
Sont envolées ces croix
Chanter la gloire de leurs morts

      Le jour de la Victoire
      Tous les peuples chanteront

      Et les mers
      Se changeront en miel

Soldats
    Canons

    Un ballon jette un bouquet de fleurs

Les matelots lointains

       Les matelots couleur de vieille pipe

    Chanteront à genoux sur les vagues

La Seine coulera pleine de fleurs
Et ses ponts
Seront aussi des arcs de triomphe

     LES VILLES ET LES TAMBOURS ROULENT

AEROPLANES   AEROPLANES

Won't fold their wings that morning

AEROPLANES   AEROPLANES

From which cemetery of heroes
Have these crosses flown
Singing the glory of their dead

       Victory Day
       Everyone will sing

       And the seas
       Will turn into honey

Soldiers

     Cannons

   A balloon throws out a bouquet of flowers

The far-off sailors

          Sailors the color of old pipes

    Will sing on their knees over the waves

The Seine will flow by full of flowers
And its bridges too
Will be arches of triumph

         DRUMS ROLL AND CITIES ROLL

     Et quand la nuit viendra
      Les étoiles tomberont sur la foule

Et après
Tout en haut de la Tour Eiffel
J'allume mon cigare
      Pour les astres en danger

Là-bas
   Sur la borne du monde
Quelqu'un chante un hymne de triomphe

                        And when night comes
                        Stars will fall on the crowds

And then
At the top of the Eiffel Tower
I'll light my cigar
                        For the threatened stars

Down there
                At the end of the earth
Someone's singing a triumphal hymn

TOUR EIFFEL

à Robert Delaunay

EIFFEL TOWER

for Robert Delaunay

Le Tour 1910 — PARIS
Delaunay

Tour Eiffel
Guitare du ciel

        Ta télégraphie sans fil
        Attire les mots
        Comme un rosier les abeilles

Pendant la nuit
La Seine ne coule plus

        Télescope ou clairon

        TOUR EIFFEL

Et c'est une ruche de mots
Ou un encrier de miel

Tour Eiffel
Guitare du ciel
Guitar of the sky

                Attracting words
                To your telegraphy
                Like a rosebush its bees

At night
The Seine stops flowing

                      Telescope or bugle

                        EIFFEL TOWER

It's a hive of words
An inkwell of honey

Au fond de l'aube
Une araignée aux pattes en fil de fer
Faisait sa toile de nuages

    Mon petit garçon
    Pour monter à la Tour Eiffel
    On monte sur un chanson

   Do
       ré
           mi
               fa
                   sol
                       la
                           si
                              do

    Nous sommes en haut

Un oiseau chante   C'est le vent
Dans les antennes   De l'Europe
Télégraphiques   Le vent électrique

    Là-bas

Les chapeaux s'envolent
Ils ont des ailes mais ils ne chantent pas

At the end of dawn
A spider with wire legs
Spun a web of clouds

    My boy
    To climb the Eiffel Tower
    You climb up on a song

  Do
      ré
           mi
                fa
                     sol
                         la
                             si
                                 do

      Nous sommes en haut
        We're at the top

A bird sings	It's the wind
In the telegraph	Of Europe
Antennas	The electric wind

        Down there

Hats fly off
They have wings but can't sing

Jacqueline
                Fille de France
Qu'est-ce que tu vois là-haut

La Seine dort
Sous l'ombre de ses ponts

Je vois tourner la Terre
Et je sonne mon clairon
Vers toutes les mers

        Sur le chemin
        De ton parfum
        Tous les abeilles et les paroles s'en vont

        Sur les quatre horizons
Qui n'a pas entendu cette chanson

JE SUIS LE REINE DE L'AUBE DE PÔLES
JE SUIS LA ROSE DES VENTS QUI SE FANE TOUS LES AUTOMNES
ET TOUTE PLEINE DE NEIGE
JE MEURS DE LA MORT DE CETTE ROSE
DANS ME TÊTE UN OISEAU CHANTE TOUTE L'ANNÉE

C'est comme ça qu'un jour la Tour m'a parlé

Jacqueline
                Daughter of France
What do you see up there?

The Seine's asleep
Under the shadow of its bridges

I can see the Earth turning
And I blow my bugle
To all the seas

        On the road
        Of your perfume
        All the bees and all the words take off

        On the four horizons
Who hasn't heard this song

I AM THE QUEEN OF THE DAWN OF THE POLES
I AM THE COMPASS ROSE OF THE WINDS THAT FADES EVERY FALL
AND FILLED WITH SNOW
I DIE FROM THE DEATH OF THAT ROSE
ALL YEAR LONG A BIRD SINGS INSIDE MY HEAD

That's how the Tower spoke to me one day

Tour Eiffel
Volière du monde

        Chante   Chante

Sonnerie de Paris

Le géant pendu au milieu du vide
Est l'affiche de France

        Le jour de la Victoire
        Tu la raconteras aux étoiles

Paris Août 1917.

Eiffel Tower
Aviary of the world

        Sing   Sing

Bell-clang of Paris

The giant hanging in the void
Is a poster for France

        On the day of Victory
        You'll tell it to the stars

Paris August 1917.

VERSIONES ALTERNATIVAS

VERSIONS ALTERNATIVES

ALTERNATIVE VERSIONS

ÉQUATORIALE

à Pablo Picasso

C'était le temps où s'ouvrirent mes paupières sans ailes
Et je commençai à chanter sur les horizons dénoués

Sortant de leurs nids
                Les bannières bruissent dans l'air

LES HOMMES
          ENTRE LES HERBES
                    CHERCHAIENT LES FRONTIÈRES

Sur le champ commun
                le monde meurt
Des chefs précoces
                surgissaient des ailes ardentes
Et dans la tranchée équatoriale
                brisé par intervalles

Sous l'ombre des aéroplanes vivantes
Les soldats chantaient dans les longues soirées

Les cités d'Europe
            S'éteignent une à une

Cheminant vers l'exil
Le dernier roi portait au cou
Une chaîne de lampes éteintes

            Les étoiles
                qui tombaient
            Étaient les vers luisants de la mousse

Et les affiches
            pendaient au long des murs

EQUATORIAL

for Pablo Picasso

It was the time when my eyelids opened still wingless
And I began to sing of far-off places unraveling

Leaving their nests
                    Flags stun the air

MEN
        LOOKED FOR THE BORDERLINES
                                      IN THE GRASS

The world dies
            on an ordinary field
Immature heads
            sprout flaming wings
Along the smashed stretches
                    of the equatorial trench

Under the shadows of the vivacious aeroplanes
Soldiers were singing in the hard afternoons

The cities of Europe
            Go out one by one

Walking into exile
The last king wore a chain
Of extinguished lanterns around his neck

        The stars
            that fell
        Were glowworms of moss

And posters were hanged
            along the walls

Une ombre roula sur le pente des monts
Où le vieil organiste faisait chanter les forêts

        Le vent berçait les horizons
        Accrochés aux mâts et aux voiles

Sur l'arc-en-ciel
        Un oiseau chantait

    Ouvrez-moi la montagne

Partout dans le sol
Je vis des ailes d'hirondelles
Et le Christ qui s'envola
Laissa oubliée la couronne d'épines

        Assis sur le parallèle
        Regardons notre temps

SIÈCLE ENCHAÎNÉ DANS UN ANGLE DU MONDE

En un miroir mouvant
Des barques passaient sous les ponts
Et les anges-courriers
        Reposaient dans la fumée des dreadnoughts

Dans l'herbe
        sifflait la locomotive en rut
Qui a traversé l'hiver
Les deux cordes de ses rails
Derrière d'elle restent en chantant
Comme une guitare indocile

Son œil nu
        cigare de l'horizon
                Danse entre les arbres
Elle est le Diogène à la pipe allumée
Cherchant parmi les mois et les jours

A shadow circled over the foothills
Where the ancient organist makes the forest sing

        Wind rocks horizons
        Lifted by rigging and sails

A bird sang
        Over the rainbow

    Open the mountain for me

I saw the wings of swallows
Scattered on the ground
And Christ took flight
And forgot to take his crown of thorns

        Sitting above the parallel line
        We look at our age

CENTURY CHAINED TO A CORNER OF THE WORLD

In the mirrors of the present
Boats go by under the bridges
And angel-postmen
        Rest in the smoke of the dreadnoughts

In the grass
        the locomotive that crossed the winter
Whistles in heat
The two strings of its track
Still singing
Like an untamed guitar

Its naked eye
        cigar of the horizon
                Dances in the trees
It's Diogenes with a lit pipe
Searching among the months and days

Sur le chantier equinoxial
Je commence mon voyage

Chaque étoile
               Est un obus qui éclate

Les plumes de ma gorge
Tiédirent au soleil
               qui a perdu une aile

Le divin aéroplane
Portait un rameau d'olivier entre les mains

Cependant
               Les couchants blessés saignent
Et dans le port les jours qui s'éloignaient
Portaient une croix à la place de l'ancre

En chantant asseyons-nous sur les plages

Les plus braves capitaines   Le Capitaine Cook
Sur un ice-berg vont au pôle   Chasse les aurores boréales
Pour laisser sa pipe aux lèvres   Au pôle sud
Des Esquimaux

D'autres enfoncent des lances fraîches dans le Congo

Le cœur de l'Afrique ensoleillée
S'ouvre comme les figues becquetées

Et les nègres
               de race divine
esclaves en Europe
Essuyaient de leur visage
               la neige qui les tache

I began to walk
Along the equinoctial path

Every star
   A bursting shell

The feathers of my throat
Cooled by the sun
    that had lost a wing

The divine aeroplane
Brought an olive branch in its hands

And yet
   Wounded sunsets are still bleeding
And the days set off from the harbor
Carrying a cross instead of an anchor

We sit singing on the beaches

The most courageous captains	Captain Cook
Left on an iceberg to the poles	Hunts aurora borealises
To stick their pipes	At the South Pole
In Eskimo lips	

Others plant fresh lances in the Congo

The sunstruck heart of Africa
Opens like pecked figs

And Negroes
    of the divine race
slaves in Europe
Washed off the snow
    that stained their faces

Des hommes aux ailes courtes
       Ont tout parcouru
Et un noble explorateur de Norvège
A rapporté à l'Europe
Comme butin de guerre
       entre rares animaux
Et arbres exotiques
Les quatre points cardinaux

Je me suis embarqué aussi
Laissant mon écueil je suis venu vous voir

Les mouettes volaient autour de mon chapeau

Et me voilà
    debout
       sur d'autres baies

Sous le bocage aphone
Passent lentement
      les cités esclaves
Cousues une à une par les fils téléphoniques

Et les paroles et les gestes
Volent autour du télégraphe
Se brûlant les ailes
      tels des dieux inexperts

Les aéroplanes fatigués
Vont se poser sur les paratonnerres

Les biplanes, enceinte,
      enfanteront au vol dans le brouillard

Ils sont les oiseaux aimés
Qui ont chanté dans nos cages

C'est l'oiseau qui s'endort ente les branches
Sans cacher sa tête sous son aile

Men with clipped wings
                          Have overrun everything
And a noble explorer from Norway
Brought back to Europe
As the spoils of war
                        along with the rare animals
And exotic trees
The four cardinal points

And I too have embarked
Leaving my reef I came to see you

Seagulls flew around my hat

And here I am
               standing
                           in other bays

Under the voiceless trees
The captive cities
                slowly go by
Sewn to one another by telephone wires

And words and faces
Fly around the telegraph
Burning their wings
                        like inexperienced gods

Exhausted aeroplanes
Went off to rest on the lightning rods

Biplanes in labor
                  give birth flying through the fog

They are the love birds
That sang in our cages

The bird that sleeps in the branches
Without tucking its head under its wing

Dans les nuits
              les avions volent autour du phare
Le phare qui agonise au fond des années

Quelqu'un affligé
              Les pupiles vides
Lançant à la mer ses tristes jours
Prend la barque

Partir
            Et de là-bas très loin
Regarder les fenêtres éclairées
Et les ombres qui traversent les miroirs

Comme une bande
              de jeunes hirondelles
Les émigrants chantent sur les flots soulevés

MER

MER DES FUMÉES VERTES

Je voudrais cette mer pour ma soif d'antan

Pleine de flottantes chevelures

Sur ses flots s'en allèrent mes réelles angoisses

Sous les eaux mousseuses
                Un séraphin naufragé
                Tisse des couronnes d'algues

La nouvelle lune
            avec les mâts tronqués
Mouille à Marseille ce matin

Et les plus vieux marins
Dans le fond de la fumée de leurs pipes
Ont rencontré des perles vivantes

At night
   the planes flew by the lighthouse
The lighthouse dying at the end of the years

Someone embittered
     Empty eyes
Takes a boat
Casting his sad days into the sea

To leave
   And from there far-off
To see the lit windows
And the shadows that cross the mirrors

Like a flock
   of young swallows
Emigrants were singing on the inverted waves

SEA

SEA OF GREEN CLOUDS OF SMOKE

I wanted that sea for my old thirst

Full of floating strands of hair

On those waves they were my true desires

Under the gaseous water
     A shipwrecked seraphim
     Weaves crowns of seaweed

The new moon
    with its rigging broken
Anchored in Marseilles this morning

And the most ancient sailors
Found living pearls
At the bottom of their pipe smoke

Le capitaine du sous-marin
Oublia au fond son destin

De retour à la terre
                Il a vu qu'un autre portait son étoile

Exilés fiévreux de la vieille planète
Tués en s'envolant
Par les canons antiaériens

Un émigrant aveugle
                     Traîne quatre lions maîtrisés
Un autre porte l'hôpital du port
Un rossignol désaccordé

Ce jeune pilote
          qui oublie sa pipe fumante
Près du volcan éteint
Rencontra dans la ville
                Les hommes agenouillés
Et vit accoucher les Vierges

Là-bas
                          là-bas

Viennent pensifs
         les chercheurs d'or
Ils passent en chantant entre les feuilles
Sur leurs épaules
Ils portent la Californie

Au fond du crépuscule
Venaient les mendiants demi-muets

Un murmure de prière
                Incline les arbres

        Sur les mers
      fuit l'Été

The submarine captain
In the depths forgot his mission

Returning to land
                    He saw that someone else was wearing his star

Feverish exiles from the old planet
That was killed on take-off
By anti-aircraft guns

A blind emigrant
                    Brought four trained lions
And another took a nightingale that was out of tune
To the harbor hospital

That boy pilot
            who left his smoking pipe
Near the extinct volcano
Found men on their knees
                        In the city
And saw pregnant virgins giving birth

There far-off
                            there far-off

Pensive gold prospectors come
                        singing among the leaves
Carrying California
On their shoulders

Half-mute beggars came
Through the depths of twilight

The murmur of someone praying
                          Bowed the trees over

            Summertime fled
        over the seas

QUE DE CHOSES J'AI VUES !

Entre la brume végétale et épaisse
Les mendiants des rues de Londres
Collés comme des affiches
Contre les murs froids

Je me souviens
                Je me souviens

Ce soir de Printemps
Une jeune fille malade
Quittant ses petites ailes à la porte
Entra à l'hôpital

Cette même nuit
                sous le ciel concave
Dix zeppelins vinrent à Paris
Et un chasseur de sangliers
En laissa sept saignants
Sur l'aube agreste

Dans la nuée qu'effleure le toit

Une horloge verte
                Annonce l'année

1917

PLUIE

                Sous l'eau
                Nous enterrerons les morts

      Quelqu'un qui pleurait
      Faisait tomber les feuilles

WHAT THINGS I'VE SEEN !

In the thick and vegetal fog
Beggars on the streets of London
Stuck like posters
Against the frigid walls

I remember it well
               I remember

That afternoon in Spring
A girl who was ill
Left her two wings at the door
And went into the sanatorium

That same night
             under the oblong sky
Ten Zeppelins arrived in Paris
And a hunter of wild boars
Left seven bleeding
In the country dawn

In the cloud that brushes the roof

A green clock
             Announces the year

1917

IT'S RAINING

                        They buried the dead
                        Underwater

              Someone weeping
              Made the leaves fall

Il y a des signes dans le ciel
Dit l'astrologue barbu
                Une pomme et une étoile
                Que becquètent les hiboux

Mars
        passe au travers du
                Sagittaire

LA LUNE SE LÈVE

                Un astre outragé
                se glisse

Astrologues aux mitres pointues
De ses barbes tombent des flocons de cendre

Et me voilà ici
        dans les bois accordés
Plus savamment que les vieilles harpes

Dans la maison
        qui pend du vide
Fatigués de chercher
        les Rois Mages se sont endormis

Les ascenseurs reposent accroupis

Et dans toutes les alcôves
Chaque fois que sonne l'heure
Sort de l'horloge un page sévère
Comme pour dire
        La voiture attend
                Madame

Près de la porte ouverte
Le nègre esclave
        ouvre vivement la bouche

There are signs in the sky
Says the bearded astrologer
                          Owls are pecking
                          An apple and a star

Mars
          passes through
                      Sagittarius

THE MOON COMES OUT
                          A mistreated star
                          slips away

Flakes of ashes fell from the beards
Of astrologers in pointy miters

And here I am
            in forests
More expertly tuned than old harps

In the house
            that hangs in the void
Tired of searching
            the Three Kings have gone to sleep

Elevators squatting doze

And in every bedroom
When it strikes the hour
A reliable bellhop comes out of the clock
As if to say
            The car is waiting
                    Madam

Next to the open door
The negro slave
            quickly opens his mouth

Pour le maître pianiste
Qui fait chanter ses dents

Ce soir j'ai vu
Les dernières affiches phonographiques
C'était une confusion de cris
Et de chants aussi divers
Que dans les ports étrangers

Les hommes de demain
Viendront déchiffrer les hiéroglyphes
Que nous laissons à présent
Écrits à l'envers
Entre les fers de la Tour Eiffel

Nous arrivons à la fin de la mêlée
Mon horloge a perdu toutes ses heures

Je te parcours lentement
Siècle coupé en deux
      Et avec un pont
Sur un fleuve ensanglanté
Chemin de l'Occident

Un soir
   au fond de la vie
Passe un horizon de chameaux
Sur leurs épaules mobiles
Entre deux pyramides osseuses
Les hommes de l'Égypte
Pleurent comme de jeunes crocodiles

Et les saints en train
      cherchant d'autres régions
Montaient à toutes les stations

Mon âme sœur des trains

    Un train peut s'égrener comme un rosaire
    La croix lumineuse parfume les plaines

For the master pianist
Who can make his teeth sing

This afternoon I've seen
The latest phonographic notices
A riot of screams
And songs as sundry
As those in foreign ports

The men of tomorrow
Will decipher the hieroglyphs
We've left
Written backwards
On the girders of the Eiffel Tower

We've reached the end of the skirmish
My watch lost its time

I travel slowly through you
Century cut in half
                      And on a bridge
Over a bloody river
I walk from the West

One afternoon
                deep in life
A horizon of camels passed by
On their mute backs
Between two bony pyramids
The men of Egypt
Weep like newborn crocodiles

On the train the saints
                    looking for other territories
Get on and off at every station

My sister soul of the trains

           A train can pray to itself like a rosary
           The smoking cross that perfumed the plains

Nous sommes ici voyageant avec les saints

Le train est un morceau de la ville qui s'éloigne

L'annonciateur des stations
A crié
       Printemps
        sur le côté gauche
          trente minutes

Un train passa plein de fleurs de fruits

Le Niagara a mouillé mes cheveux
Et une brume naît autour d'eux

Les fleuves
    Tous les fleuves des naissantes chevelures
Les rivières mal tressées
Que les ardents étés ont baisées!

Un paquebot perdu côtoie
Les îles d'or de la Voie Lactée

La Cordillère andine
      Rapide comme un convoi
Traverse l'Amérique Latine

L'Amour
        l'Amour

En peu de lieux je l'ai rencontré
Et tous les fleuves non explorés
Sous mes bras ont passé

Un matin
    les bergères des Alpes
Jouaient du violon sur la Suisse

Here we are traveling with saints

A train is a piece of the city that pushes off

The conductor
Shouted
      Spring
       exit on the left
         30 minutes

The train goes by full of flowers and fruit

Niagara Falls has drenched my hair
And a mist rises around it

The rivers
    All the rivers of rising hair
The badly braided rivers
That burning summers have kissed

A lost steamer was coasting along
The golden islands of the Milky Way

The Andes mountains
        Swift as a convoy
Crosses Latin America

Love
        Love

In few places I've found it
All the unexplored rivers
Have passed beneath my hands

One morning
       mountaineer shepherds
Played the violin over Switzerland

Et dans l'étoile voisine
Celle qui n'a pas de mains
Avec les ailes joue du piano

Le Siècle s'est embarqué sur des aéroplanes ivres

     OÙ IRAS-TU

Cheminant vers l'exil
Le dernier roi portait au cou
Une chaîne de lampes éteintes

Et hier je vis morte entre les roses
L'améthyste de Rome

ALFA
     OMEGA

   DÉLUGE
         ARC-EN-CIEL

Combien de fois la vie aura recommencé

Qui dira tout ce qui s'est passé dans un astre

    Poursuivons notre marche
    Portant la tête mure entre nos mains

LE ROSSIGNOL MÉCANIQUE A CHANTÉ

Cette multitude de mains rudes
Porte des couronnes funéraires
Vers les champs de bataille

    Quelqu'un passa perdu dans son cigare

     QUI EST-CE

And on the star next door
The one who had no hands
Played the piano with his wings

Century embarked on drunken aeroplanes

        WHERE ARE YOU GOING

Walking into exile
The last king wore a chain of extinguished lanterns
Around his neck

And yesterday I saw the amethyst of Rome
Dead among the roses

ALPHA
                                  OMEGA

              FLOOD
                                      RAINBOW

How many times will life have to begin again

Who will tell everything that has happened on a star

        We continue our march
        Carrying the ripened head in our hands

THE MECHANICAL NIGHTINGALE HAS SUNG

That throng of rough hands
Carrying funeral wreaths
To the battlefields

    Someone went by lost in his cigar

        WHO IS IT

Une main coupée
Laissa sur les marbres
La ligne équatoriale récemment poussait

Siècle
        Submerge-toi dans le soleil
Quand le soir venu
          Il atterrit au camp d'aviation

Vers le seul aéroplane
Qui chantera un jour dans l'azur
Se lèvera des années
Une volée de mains

CROIX DU SUD

SUPRÊME SIGNE   AVION DU CHRIST

L'enfant rougissant sous ses ailes nues
Viendra avec le clairon entre les doigts
Le clairon encore frais qui annoncera
La fin de l'Univers

A severed hand
Left the new equatorial line
On the marble

Century
        Sink into the sun
When in the evening
           It lands at the airfield

A flock of hands
Will rise from the years
Toward the one aeroplane
That will sing someday in the blue

THE SOUTHERN CROSS

THE SUPREME SIGN   THE CHRIST AIRLINER

The rosy child with bare wings
Will come with his bugle in his hands
The brand-new bugle that heralds
The End of the Universe

TOUR EIFFEL

À Max Jacob

Tour Eiffel
Guitare du ciel

Ta télégraphie sans fil
Attire les mots
Comme un rosier les abeilles

Pendant la nuit
La Seine ne coule plus

Tour Eiffel
Ruche des mots
Encrier de miel

Araignée aux pattes en fil de fer
Qui fait sa toile de nuages

Mon petit garçon
On monte sur un chanson

Do
      ré
           mi
                 fa
                     sol
                         la
                             si
                                 do

EIFFEL TOWER

For Max Jacob

Eiffel Tower
Guitar of the sky

Attracting words
To your telegraphy
Like a rosebush its bees

At night
The Seine stops flowing

Eiffel Tower
Hive of words
Inkwell of honey

Spider with wire legs
That spins a web of clouds

My boy
You climb up on a song

Do
     ré
          mi
               fa
                    sol
                        la
                            si
                                do

Nous sommes en haut
Télégraphie sans fil
Vent électrique
La Seine dort sous l'ombre de ses ponts

La parole et les abeilles
Vont dans l'air
Par un chemin
De parfum

Tour Eiffel
Boîte prodigieuse
Sonnerie de Paris
Affiche de France

Le jour de la Victoire
Tu la crieras aux étoiles

We're at the top
Wireless telegraphy
Electric wind
The Seine's asleep under the shadow of its bridges

Words and bees
Go off through the air
On a road
Of perfume

Eiffel Tower
Box of wonders
Bell-clang of Paris
Poster for France

On the day of Victory
You'll shout it out to the stars

TORRE EIFFEL

Torre Eiffel
Guitara del cielo

        Tu telegrafía sin hilos
        Atrae las palabras
        Como un rosal les abejas

Durante la noche
Y no corre el Sena
        Telescopio o clarín
        Torre Eiffel
Y es una colmena de palabras
O un tintero de miel

        En el fondo del alba
        Una araña de patas de alambre
        Urdía su tela de nubes

        Mi niño
        Para subir a la Torre Eiffel
        Se trepa por una canción
        do
           ré
              mi
                 fa
              sol
                la
                   si
                      do
        Ya estamos arriba

EIFFEL TOWER

Tour Eiffel
Guitar of the sky
           Attracting words
           To your telegraphy
           Like a rosebush its bees

At night
The Seine stops flowing
           Telescope or bugle
           Eiffel Tower
It's a hive of words
An inkwell of honey

           At the end of dawn
           A spider with wire legs
           Spun a web of clouds

           My boy
           To climb the Eiffel Tower
           You climb up on a song
           do
              ré
                mi
                    fa
                        sol
                            la
                              si
                                do
           We're at the top

Un pájaro canta
En las antenas
Telegráficas

        Es el viento
        De Europa
        El viento eléctrico

        Allá abajo
Los sombreros vuelan
Tienen alas pero no cantan
Jacobina
        Hija de Francia
Que ves allá en lo alto

El Sena duerme
Bajo la sombra de los puentes
Veo girar la tierra
Toco el clarín
Para todos las mares
        Sobre el camino
        De tu perfume
        Todas las abejas et palabras se van

        En los cuatro horizontes
        Quién no oyó este cantar

YO SOY LA REINA DEL ALBA DE LOS POLOS
YO SOY LA ROSA DE LOS VIENTOS QUE SE MARCHITA CADA OTOÑO
Y TODA LLENA DE NIEVE
MUERO DE LA MUERTE DE ESA ROSA
EN MI CABEZA UN PÁJARO CANTA TODO EL AÑO

A bird sings
In the telegraph
Antennas

        It's the wind
        Of Europe
        The electric wind

        Down there
Hats fly off
They have wings but can't sing
Jacobina
        Daughter of France
What do you see up there?

The Seine's asleep
Under the shadow of its bridges
I can see the Earth turning
And I blow my bugle
To all the seas
        On the road
        Of your perfume
        All the bees and all the words take off

        On the four horizons
        Who hasn't heard this song

I AM THE QUEEN OF THE DAWN OF THE POLES
I AM THE COMPASS ROSE OF THE WINDS THAT FADES EVERY FALL
AND FILLED WITH SNOW
I DIE FROM THE DEATH OF THAT ROSE
ALL YEAR LONG A BIRD SINGS INSIDE MY HEAD

Así un día me habló la torre
Torre Eiffel
Jaula del mundo
Canta
               Canta

Repique de París

El gigante colgado en medio del vacío
Es el cartel de Francia

               El día de la victoria
               Tú se lo contarás a las estrellas

That's how the Tower spoke to me one day
Eiffel Tower
Aviary of the world
Sing
                Sing

Bell-clang of Paris

The giant hanging in the void
Is a poster for France

                On the day of Victory
                You'll tell it to the stars

NOTES

El espejo de agua. Poemas 1915–1916

This chapbook was said by the author to have been published by Biblioteca Orión in Buenos Aires in 1916—presumably around the same time that his collection, *Adán* [Adam, written in 1914] appeared in Santiago—prior to Huidobro's arrival in Europe. Only a couple of copies seem to be extant, and are now in the possession of the Fundación Huidobro, having been previously in the hands of the author in one case, and his eldest daughter in the other, although Huidobro's biographer Volodia Teitelboim also mentions one being in the collection of Braulio Arenas, poet and first editor of Huidobro's collected works. Huidobro claimed that the Orión edition was superseded by a "second edition" in Madrid in 1918, *identical with its predecessor in all respects, but with no publisher listed*; this was supposedly printed for the author by Imprenta Jesús López. There is a note in the Huidobro papers, signed by Tomás Mariñas, director of that firm, to the effect that he had printed this second edition in June 1918 "exactamente igual al ejemplar de la primera edición del mismo libro, publicado in Buenos Aires y traído aquí como modelo por el Sr. Huidobro" [*exactly the same as the copy of the first edition of the same book, published in Buenos Aires and brought here as a master copy by Mr Huidobro*].[1] A third and final edition, reset, appeared later the same year and is the one known to posterity.

There was a furore a couple of years later over the veracity of the Argentinian edition, with Huidobro being accused of having antedated the information in the Madrid edition, in order to bolster his claim to being the founder of Creationism. Pierre Reverdy likewise claimed responsibility for that movement's founding and the two poets, previously friends and colleagues, fell out over the affair. Scholarship today varies, and I long adhered to the belief that the author had been unfairly maligned, but further reading—especially in the thorough analysis of the affair by Waldo Rojas[2]—now inclines me to assume that the alleged "third edition" is in fact the real first edition of this volume. I will leave it there, noting only

---

[1] Vicente Huidobro, *Obra poética*, ed. Cedomil Goic, Paris: ALLCA, 2003, p.384
[2] Waldo Rojas, 'El fechado dudoso de *El Espejo de Agua* a la luz de la tentativa poética francesa de Vicente Huidobro. ¿Un extravío del anhelo de originalidad radical?' in *Caravelle*, n°82, Toulouse, 2004, pp. 63-88. Rojas also edited Huidobro's collected poems in French in 1998.

that most of the commentaries I have seen have failed to offer the kind of strict comparative analysis required, and have tended to be driven, or so it would appear, by a desire to exculpate the author. In any event, the whole incident was a decidedly minor hiccup in literary history, even if it did lead to Reverdy and Huidobro ending their friendship. *El espejo de agua* is clearly a transitional work, in a different style to that employed in *Adán*, but not as radical as the work which was to follow in the other publications from 1917 and 1918. It is quite possible that the poems in it do in fact date from 1915–16.

Five of the poems were translated into French, with the extensive help of others, and published in 1917 in the magazine *Nord-Sud*: 'El hombre triste' (according to Cedomil Goic in the *Obra poética*, the handwriting in the manuscript of this poem appears to be Reverdy's), 'Otoño', 'Nocturno', 'Nocturno II' and 'Alguien iba a nacer'. These and two more then appeared in the volume *Horizon carré* [*Square Horizon*, also available in this series of Shearsman editions], while the poem 'El espejo de agua' was to appear in *Saisons choisies*, a selected poems in French, in 1921, thus leaving only 'Arte poética' unpublished in French translation.

Ecuatorial

This poem was written in March/April 1918 and was published in August of the same year by Imprenta Juan Pueyo, Madrid, as a limited-edition chapbook. The entire text was then reprinted in the Madrid magazine *Cervantes* in July 1919, albeit in a restricted layout, eschewing the expansive field-composition of the original, and containing a number of errors. A second edition only appeared in 1978 in Santiago, edited by Óscar Hahn, and was based on the Spanish edition, although, in the interim, the text had been reprinted in two separate collected editions of Huidobro's work. For the second edition of this translation we have re-set the poem to align more closely with the first edition, a facsimile of which is now available from the Biblioteca Nacional de Chile.

Hallali

This chapbook was published in Madrid by Imprenta Jesús López in 1918. Spanish versions of the poems appeared in the magazine *Cervantes* in July 1919, in translations by Rafael Cansinos Asséns. The poems have only been republished since in collected editions.

Hallali—the word exists in both French and English—is the bugle signal to advance, used for the cavalry, mounted hunters and, here, foot soldiers in the trenches.

Tour Eiffel

Tour Eiffel first appeared in a more traditional left-adjusted layout in Reverdy's magazine *Nord-Sud* in the August–September 1917 issue, with a dedication to Max Jacob. It then appeared as a splendid chapbook in Madrid in 1918, published by Imprenta Juan Pueyo, where it gained its now-familiar spatial organisation. This chapbook also benefited from paper stock in four different colours, a cover image by Robert Delaunay (now the dedicatee of the poem) and a tipped-in reproduction of Delaunay's painting *La Tour*, of 1910, which we have reproduced here on the section-title page. Delaunay produced a series of paintings of the Tower over the period 1910–1912 in a style described as *simultanéisme*, best regarded as a variant of Cubism.

Copies of the chapbook are in a number of art galleries, and a (*not completely* accurate) facsimile was included as an insert with the special Huidobro issue of *Poesía*, edited by René de Costa, triple issue 30, 31 & 32, Madrid, 1989. The latter is indispensable for admirers of Huidobro's work.

The first edition may be viewed online on Princeton University's website: https://graphicarts.princeton.edu/2018/03/27/robert-delaunay-and-vicente-huidobro/

Appendix: Alternative Versions

Équatoriale

There is a French version of the first 81 lines of *Ecuatorial* in manuscript, which, according to Cedomil Goic in the 2003 *Obra poética*, may well be in the hand of Picasso, while another exists of the complete poem, but lacking the field layout of the first edition. This was not published until the *Obra poética*, albeit being re-set there, not entirely accurately, to accord with the layout of the Spanish version. We reprint that version here in the second edition of the current volume, but we follow the layout of the Spanish first edition printed earlier in this book. We have eliminated a few punctuation marks that appear to be superfluous, and have also made some minor orthographic corrections in the case of mis-spellings in the French text, but have preserved the somewhat erratic use of capitalisation. The identity of the translator is unconfirmed, although it is clear that other Spanish poems from this period were translated into French by the author himself with the aid of, variously, Pierre Reverdy, Francis Picabia, Juan Gris, and others. It is likely that this is the case again here, although the complete truth is unlikely ever to be discovered.

Tour Eiffel

The first version here is the original *Nord-Sud* version referred to on the previous page. The Spanish translation which follows is the text published in the anthology *Índice de la nueva poesía americana* (Mexico City & Buenos Aires: El Inca Ediciones, 1926), edited by Alberto Hidalgo, with the assistance of Jorge Luis Borges and Huidobro. Although uncredited in that volume, the translation appears to be the same as that published in the magazines *Cervantes* (Madrid, 1919) and *Ariel* (Santiago, 1925), where it is ascribed to Rafael Cansinos Asséns, the Madrid-based writer and critic who had met Huidobro on his first forays into the city. Cansinos Asséns was a significant figure in the city's literary circles at the time and helped Huidobro's work gain traction. The text's layout varies slightly from the appearance in *Cervantes*, and contains one peculiarity: the name *Jacqueline* in the original French has metamorphosed into *Jacobina*. We have no way of knowing if this is the result of a transcription error, or an actual change made by the author.

Tony Frazer

The Translator

Eliot Weinberger's books of literary essays include *Karmic Traces, An Elemental Thing,* and *The Ghosts of Birds*. His political articles are collected in *What I Heard About Iraq* and *What Happened Here: Bush Chronicles*. The author of *19 Ways of Looking at Wang Wei*, he is a translator of the poetry of Bei Dao, the editor of *The New Directions Anthology of Classical Chinese Poetry*, and the general editor of the series *Calligrams: Writings from and on China*. Among his translations of Latin American literature are *The Poems of Octavio Paz*, Jorge Luis Borges' *Selected Non-Fictions*, Vicente Huidobro's *Altazor*, and Xavier Villaurrutia's *Nostalgia for Death*. His work regularly appears in the *London Review of Books* and has been translated into over thirty languages.

www.ingramcontent.com/pod-product-compliance
Lightning Source LLC
Chambersburg PA
CBHW031400160426
43196CB00007B/840